C000108361

MY HEART IN YOUR HANDS

JENNIFER CHAPMAN

Grosvenor House
Publishing Limited

All rights reserved
Copyright © Jennifer Chapman, 2020

The right of Jennifer Chapman to be identified as the author of this
work has been asserted in accordance with Section 78
of the Copyright, Designs and Patents Act 1988

The book cover is copyright to Jennifer Chapman

This book is published by
Grosvenor House Publishing Ltd
Link House
140 The Broadway, Tolworth, Surrey, KT6 7HT.
www.grosvenorhousepublishing.co.uk

This book is sold subject to the conditions that it shall not, by way of
trade or otherwise, be lent, resold, hired out or otherwise circulated
without the author's or publisher's prior consent in any form of binding or
cover other than that in which it is published and
without a similar condition including this condition being imposed
on the subsequent purchaser.

A CIP record for this book
is available from the British Library

ISBN 978-1-83975-249-0

To my children;
You give me strength, meaning and
the deepest happiness
You are my everything
I love you so very much

Contradiction

With every eruption of excitement,
Comes an immense amount of fear.

Never have I felt so needed,
Yet with your tears so rejected.

That I have learnt so much,
Yet have so much more to learn.

That my life is complete,
Yet have everything to work towards.

Achievement has never felt so great,
While simultaneously having everything to prove.

With tears that only I can render,
Yet one tear feels inconsolable.

Life has become a balancing act,
With every move incased by fragility,
One false move and everything could break.

I give to you

I give to you my heart until the very last beat it takes,
I give to you my love until the world around us breaks,
I give to you my soul from the very deepest place,
I give to you my strength for every problem that you face.
I give to you my world because that's what you gave to me,
From the second you were born until the end of eternity.

Other people

'O, isn't she just gorgeous',
The strangers in the street rejoice,
'It's a boy' I retort back,
Suppressing the anger in my voice.

'Doesn't he look content',
Say the people who haven't got a clue,
'Apart from all the screaming' I think,
'…Content' I smile, 'that's true'.

'Is he sleeping through the night?'
People try to empathize,
'Clearly not' I want to say,
Judging by the bags that are under my eyes.

'Are you enjoying maternity leave?'
'And having a bit of a rest'
Ask the people who have never had children,
Not knowing that everyday is like a test.

'Are you back in your pre-pregnancy jeans?'
Ask those who seem to want to make you cry.
'Nearly' I respond back,
Knowing this is a complete lie.

Despite their best intentions,
And wanting to help or just be nice,
There is a sinking feeling inside me,
When people offer their advice!

Sleepless nights

When your cries at night break through the silence,
The reason for your awakening not always clear,
And my eyes feel heavy and my body weak,
I plead with you to sleep.

In that same moment your eyes meet mine,
And the answer to the absent question is clear,
I would rather have a sleepless night to share with you,
Than a restful night alone.

Silence of the night

In the silence of the night,
The darkness surrounds me like a blanket,
I listen to your breathing,
Rapid, then slow, then silence.

Awaiting gingerly your next gasp of air,
The seconds between each breath a never-ending eternity,
I exhale in tandem with you,
Realising that I too have held my breath.

The hours feel like minutes,
As I watch your chest rise and fall,
And it's almost incomprehensible,
Your presence impossible to process.

The waves of love engulf me,
And the piece of my life
That I didn't even know was missing,
Is now complete.

No words

He speaks no words
Yet he teaches me everything there is to know about love.

Just one tiny kiss

Hours spent rocking to tempt your slumber,
With your eyes getting heavy I beg sleep not to encumber.
Pacing the landing walking up and down,
You gaze at me smiling with a crooked little frown.
The clock strikes a time that barely seems real,
You giggle and gurgle offering all but a squeal.

Slowly you enter the world of dreams,
Your eyes gently closing – sleep is nigh it seems.
Placing you down my arms feel so bare,
I miss you already although you're right there.
Staring at you in wonder I am swamped with love,
I'm sure one little kiss won't wake you up.

Quick as a flash your eyes spring open,
With one tiny kiss you have awoken.
I take my cue and start the process again,
The muscles in my arms ache where you've lain,
Yet it's a mistake I know I'll continue to make,
As I love you so much I think my heart may break.

Cast iron bubbles

The world engulfs us,
Swallowing us so quickly that to those around us it goes unnoticed.
Walking down the road in our own protective bubble,
A bubble that has its own agenda
A front of calm and contentedness,
Of joy and togetherness.

Very quickly the transparency of its surface becomes brick,
A wall behind which lies assumed tranquility.
Its existence rarely questioned, yet rarely entered.
As who would choose to disturb serenity?
The softness of the bubble turning from brick to iron,
Impenetrable to those around it.

The space inside slowly shrinking,
Its weight becoming heavier as the walls thicken.
A space filled so much with love,
Love, wonder and silent bonding.
Yet with silence comes isolation, fear and confusion,
Just yearning for someone to penetrate the walls enough to allow
Just some of the world in.

Overwhelming

Every day I love you,
And every time I look at you,
I fall in love with you more.
Some days the love is overwhelming,
So much so that I literally catch my breath.
I hold you in my arms and can't help but cry,
Never realizing until now that love could be so intense,
So overpowering and so paralyzing.
Holding you close to me,
I don't notice the time pass,
Chores stack up and tasks are left undone,
Yet I only want to stay in this moment,
Treasure it and let it consume me.
And for all the jobs that should have filled my time,
In the time I get to spend with you,
I gain the only thing that truly matters.
Your love.

Family

Family is not a given, it is earnt,
The titles of Aunt, Uncle, Grandparent and Parent,
Are fought for, respected, and worked towards.
They are valued and given meaning,
And only when such titles are seen as privileges,
Can their meaning be truly appreciated.

Every moment of every day I work hard to earn my position as
    your Parent,
Protecting you from those who abuse their title and who take it
    for granted,
Who don't give you the love that comes with the honor of being
    in your life,
Who assume that their familial position affords them a title,
And use it in name only when it suits them yet not in action.

My role as your Parent means I shall teach you the value of family,
Of respecting those who respect you,
And allowing you to see that honorable titles such as Aunt and
    Uncle,
Can be awarded to those who show you the unconditional regard
    you deserve,
Ensuring you feel no guilt at disregarding those who
    undeservedly assume a title,
That they have no right to hold.

The break not taken

I beg you to take him to give me a break,
I've been up so long I can hardly stay awake,
Just for an hour while I spend some time in bed,
To rest my body and my very weary head.

Yet as soon as you take him the absence is clear,
And I know right away that I just want him near.
So I follow you around while you hold him tight,
The break so yearned for now doesn't feel right.

His nappy it wet and I ask you to change him,
A job I am tired of and that can be quite grim.
'That's fine' you reply 'just don't interfere'
'I'm not' I respond, yet still I am here.

I sit down beside where the baby is lain,
And get out wipes, 'you're interfering again'.
I smile in response as I put on his clean nappy,
'I'm sure taking over seems to make you so happy'.

I ask you to dress him while I get on with some chores,
'Any outfit is fine just have a look in his drawers'.
You smile at me laughing as you take the baby away,
Knowing your chosen outfit won't be right for that day.

Ten minutes later you return looking stressed,
It's freezing outside yet our son's in only a vest.
'I've changed him three times and all would have been wrong.
Just tell me which outfit so we can all get along'.

Being a Mum is a switch that cannot be unplugged,
Even when you want it to it's like you've been drugged.
Your needs become secondary to the addiction of love,
Whatever your desires, your child's will come above.

Sometimes

Sometimes I sit and cry,
Paralysed with the fear that my best is not enough,
Or that my best was so bad
You never knew I'd tried.

Stop

In a world so full of technology and always rushing around,
With lives that are so busy our feet don't touch the ground,
There is a danger that if we don't take a minute to slow down,
We will miss all that is important in this world in which we drown.

Being a parent is a gift and one we should not waste,
You only get one chance, don't let it pass in haste.
To watch your child grow up is an honor not to be taken for granted,
Embrace every second and create memories that will remain candid.

Photos are not the only way that a memory can be preserved,
The most precious moments remain in your heart never to be
    disturbed.
The sound of a baby's laughter need not be recorded,
As in your mind it will forever ring as a sound that won't get
    thwarted.

So turn off the television and focus on the moment,
Leave your phone in a different room and act in pure bestowment.
No amount of pictures can capture touch or feeling,
Or the unspoken connection as you watch your baby sleeping.

Promise not to be the mum that is looking at her phone,
When your child is trying to show you crafts they have made all
    on their own.
Don't be the parent who is so busy you greet your child with silence,
While ignoring the little eyes who look to you for guidance.

When looking in your eyes your baby wants to see your love,
Your reassurance and encouragement is all they will dream of.
They want to hear your voice whenever they are scared,
And to know their precious moments with you they will have
    shared.

A new language

Sometimes I get things wrong,
But know my intentions are always true.
My only ever hope,
Is to do my best by you.

You try and tell me what you want
but sometimes I don't understand.
I give you milk instead of change your nappy,
Stroke your head instead of hold your hand.

I take you to the park
Thinking you'll like the swings and slide.
But really all you wanted was a cuddle,
And my arms in which to hide.

I hold you closely to me
So you know that you're secure.
Yet it seems what you actually wanted,
Was to explore the world some more.

Together we are learning
A language between just me and you
Some things will get lost in translation
But the strength of our love will always come through.

Unspoken bond

Your hand rests on mine,
Like a warmth that radiates through me,
An unspoken connection between us,
Cemented with one touch.

Your arms flail around as you sleep,
Frantically searching for the end of a nightmare,
The end only found when your hand rests on my cheek,
Proof that no words need be spoken for you to know I'm here.

Your legs sway beneath you,
Fighting to keep your balance,
Hands wrapped firmly around my fingers,
Your confidence shines in the knowledge I will never let you fall.

Never

Never is a moment wasted,
If it's a moment spent loving a child.

Maternity leave

A whole year off,
So much we can do,
Play games in the park,
See animals at the zoo.

While you're sleeping,
I can get things done,
Tick things off my 'To Do' List,
Achieve things one by one.

I can sort out all the photos,
Publish a book,
Learn a new language,
Become a fantastic cook.

It's scary how quickly,
The time has flown past,
Our year nearly over,
How has it gone so fast?

We have been to the park
And we have been to the Zoo
The things on my list
Remain as 'To Do'.

Why did I think,
That once you arrived,
I would care about
My 'To Do' List pride,

For while you have slept,
I have watched you in awe,
The things on my list,
Not mattering anymore.

I would happily trade,
For more time off with you,
All future 'ticks'
And leave tasks left 'To Do'.

Challenges

I don't like to say it,
But sometimes it's true,
You're really hard work,
And I'm knackered right through.

You're on the move,
And want to explore,
Nothing I can do,
Stops you going through that door.

A thousand toys,
With which you can play,
But you can reach my coffee,
And that's more fun any day!

You appear to like your food,
So I try and give you more,
That doesn't seem to stop you,
Then throwing it on the floor.

Walking is fun,
You're high off the ground,
But I've lost count of the bruises,
On you I seem to have found.

You appear to choose carefully,
When to bump your head,
Like when we see the doctor,
With a lump that's bright red.

The best days ever,
Are the days we share,
And even though I'm shattered,
I just don't care.

What you don't know

When you hold your arms up to me,
Awaiting a cemented embrace,
Your perfect innocence will never know,
How I too needed the security of your closeness.

When you toddle along besides me,
Your hand clasped tightly with mine,
Little do you realise,
It's me that then feels safe.

When I linger by the door,
Awaiting your wave goodbye,
Rightfully you're in the dark,
That it's not your tears I'm saving but mine.

When I pull faces to make you giggle,
And play games that make you laugh,
You are happily unaware,
Of how much your laughter completes my heart.

The perfect print

Paintbrush in hand,
Paper crisp and waiting,
Idyllic 'google' image of 'Baby's first handprint' in my head.

Intrigue on your face,
Intrigue or disinterest?
This could be more of an activity for me than you.

The ideal colour selected,
Paint delicately applied,
The perfect handprint just moments away.

Blue paint in your hair,
On the table and the floor,
Hands curled up in a tight fist that refuses to open.

A smudge of paint on the paper,
Disinterest turned active disdain,
Blue paint now mixed with the brown chocolate bribe.

The paper depicting a metaphor,
Emphasising the reality of parenthood,
Google's perfect image parallels reality yet never overlaps.

Reason

Our hands entwined,
Our eyes interlocked,
Your 'I love you mummy'
And my lost energy is revived,
My faith is restored,
And my reason for being is preserved.

Your needs

When you've had a baby your needs take second place,
At times your needs so great they are just too hard to face.
You're told the challenges are something you simply must accept,
Like now that you're a parent it's okay that you haven't slept.

Who cares if you don't eat as long as you've met your baby's needs,
And why aren't you cleaning the house in between the baby's feeds?
Who cares if you feel broken and your body and heart both hurt,
'Your baby should make it worth it' come other's replies short and
    curt.

The importance of baby bonding is told to you right away,
Who cares that you question how you feel continually throughout
    the day.
You chose to have a baby and you knew the changes that would
    bring,
Who cares if your life feels so delicate it's like you're walking
    along a string.

It's not ok you feel broken or that you haven't slept,
And it's not ok that when others have gone you've sat alone and
    wept.
It's not ok that you feel your needs don't matter anymore,
Or that you feel like a failure as you have moments you're unsure.

For anyone who tells you otherwise know it simply isn't true,
To be able to look after your children you have to look after you.
Allow yourself to collect your thoughts and to try and have a rest,
You don't need to be perfect as long as you know you're doing
    your best.

Nursery

Pulling into the carpark,
Already the guilt is there,
I'm the mum who chose work over her child,
Left her infant with strangers,
Abandoned her baby,
Put her career first.

The one who let someone else tend her baby's cries,
Walked out the door back to a childless life,
Allowed someone else to nurture her infant,
Didn't care enough to stay at home,
Failed at motherhood.

Or at least

I'm the mum who works to feed her child,
Spent hours ensuring her baby was cared for by the best,
Who wrote every inch of her child's likes and dislikes out,
So the 'strangers' could care for him,
In the way that makes him happy.

I'm the mum who works into the night,
So her waking hours are with her baby,
Feels twisted guilt whenever she and her child are apart,
Or knowing the 'strangers' are tending his tears,
When it should only ever be her.

And because of this

I'm the Mum who spends hours scared she's got it wrong,
And is constantly trying to make up for it.
The mum who cries whenever she leaves her baby,
Always questioning if this is really her best,
Or if she could have done more.

Who sits at her desk looking at your photo,
The one that takes pride of place.
Who's mind is only ever half on her job, if that,
Knowing her real life is at that time without her,
Counting down the minutes until she is home.

You made me

You've turned me into a teacher,
By asking for my advice.
Let me feel like a chef,
By saying my homecooked food is 'nice'.

You make me feel like a comedian,
By laughing at my jokes.
I've become the greatest artist,
As you admire my painting strokes.

I'm the most articulate lyricist,
As you dance to my made-up song.
You make me feel invincible,
As you need me to be strong.

You make me feel like an explorer,
Trusting me to lead the way.
I suddenly became a hairdresser,
Plaiting your hair each day.

I've become the greatest spokeswoman,
When you need me to be your voice.
Turned into a dedicated cheerleader,
With all your successes I rejoice.

I feel like a professional builder,
As I put together each toy.
Work as a high-end negotiator,
When your brother you annoy.

You turned me into a Mum,
The best job I ever had.
Even on the most difficult day,
For this job I am truly glad.

Lightning Source UK Ltd.
Milton Keynes UK
UKHW040022031220
374378UK00022B/189

9 781839 752490